World Too Loud to Hear

WORLD TOO LOUD TO HEAR

POEMS

BY

Stephen Kampa

ABLE MUSE PRESS

First published in 2023 by

Able Muse Press

www.ablemusepress.com

Printed in the United States of America

Names: Kampa, Stephen, 1981- author.
Title: World too loud to hear : poems / by Stephen Kampa.
Description: San Jose, CA : Able Muse Press, 2023.
Identifiers: LCCN 2023016585 (print) | LCCN 2023016586 (ebook) | ISBN 9781773491561 (paperback) | ISBN 9781773491578 (ebook)
Subjects: LCGFT: Poetry.
Classification: LCC PS3611.A469 W67 2023 (print) | LCC PS3611.A469 (ebook) | DDC 811/.6--dc23/eng/20230407
LC record available at https://lccn.loc.gov/2023016585
LC ebook record available at https://lccn.loc.gov/2023016586

Cover image: *Trajectory's Ending* by Rahul Shah
Cover & book design by Alexander Pepple

Able Muse Press is an imprint of *Able Muse*: A Review of Poetry, Prose & Art—at www.ablemuse.com

Able Muse Press
467 Saratoga Avenue #602
San Jose, CA 95129

Also by Stephen Kampa

Articulate as Rain (2018)
Bachelor Pad (2014)
Cracks in the Invisible (2011)

Acknowledgments

Grateful acknowledgment is made to the editors of the following publications in which these poems, or earlier versions, first appeared:

32 Poems: "Talking Heads"

ballast: "Quarterly Report on Volunteer Participation"

Bear Review: "Vectors"

Birmingham Poetry Review: "Make Jesus Great Again," "Toxin," and "Why We Remember the Martyrs"

Cincinnati Review (miCRo): "The Collectors"

Commonweal: "More Furious, More Irrefutable"

The Exacting Clam: "Well, at Least They Got One Thing Right (Including 5.8% David Kirby, 3.1% William James, 2.4% Bad Ninja, 1.8% Andrew Marvell, .6% Lee Van Cleef, .6% Jocular Lexicographer, and .1% Shakespeare)"

First Things: "The Offering"

Gargoyle: "Intro to Media Studies," "The Cards," "☆☆☆☆☆!," and "Let Me Correct You"

The Hopkins Review: "The Night I Finished Auden"

J Journal: "PSA for the NRA"

Literary Matters: "The Magician Contemplates Certain Mysteries"

Literature and Belief: "Long after Horace" and "Obligations"

Matter: "Gridlock (You Aren't Going Anywhere)" and "Performance Anxiety"

New York Quarterly: "Amazing Selling Point"

Nine Mile Magazine: "Face the Music"

Rabble Review: "Songs of Power"

Rattle: "To Keep the Day"

Red Ogre Review: "Thirteen Nearly Identical Dr. Seuss T-Shirts"

Relief: A Journal of Art and Faith: "Some Call It a Care Package, Some Call It a Sick Kit"

Shenandoah: "Candidacy" and "Healing Leaves and Unimaginable Flowers"

Stoneboat Literary Journal: "Thirteen Ways of Looking at Anger"

Tampa Review: "The Old Regret"

"Mulberries" was published in *Together in a Sudden Strangeness: America's Poets Respond to the Pandemic* (Alfred A. Knopf, 2020). My thanks to Alice Quinn, Deborah Garrison, and Todd Portnowitz for their kindness.

"Adult Party-Goers: August 15, 1929" was published in *Chasing Light* (Yellow Jacket Press, 2019), an anthology of poems inspired by photographs from the Burgert Brothers collection currently housed in the Hillsborough County Public Library. Many thanks to Allison Cadle at the library for procuring a high-quality image to work with and to Gianna Russo for her invitation and acceptance.

I owe much to the work of Jennifer Carlson, Dave Cullen, Sue Klebold, Abigail A. Kohn, Peter Langman, Matthew Lysiak, and Katherine S. Newman, who have written books on school shooters and gun culture in America. Much of my thinking on these matters, but not my errors, can be attributed to their necessary work.

Thanks are due to Mary Jo Salter and Todd Portnowitz for their perceptive readings of the manuscript, their encouragement, and their suggestions, as well as to the Amy Clampitt Fund at the Berkshire Taconic Community Foundation for giving me time and space to spread these pages all over the house until I found the book's shape.

I am grateful to Able Muse Press for allowing my work to join their excellent list. Hearty thanks to Alex Pepple for his editorial wisdom, his inexhaustible graciousness, and his eager support for this project. Hearty thanks, as well, to Amy Bagan for saving me from many a blunder and for forgiving my cussedness when it comes to any that remain.

Abigale, you make me laugh every day, and in a world like this one, that is nothing less than a miracle.

Contents

World Too Loud to Hear

Firm and irrevocable is my doom. . . .

— Shakespeare, *As You Like It*, I.iii

What shall the world do with its children?

— Robert Bly

The living, though they yearn
for consummation of their fate,
need rest, and in their turn leave
children to fulfill their doom.

— Heraclitus, trans. Brooks Haxton

World Too Loud to Hear

The Collectors

In the end, what collectors amass are stories. Stories body forth well in things.
—Lia Purpura

This explains why he had to
shoot them, each bullet a full stop at the story's end,
their stories now his stories,
the ones he tells himself over and over the way

a gun buff will lift a bright
postbellum Remington, explicate its intricate
engravings, then knock us dead
with its provenance, its uses and famous shooters,

as a means of owning it
more fully. He owns them now—the *shit they were wearing*,
their *snotty red expressions*,
their *wimp-ass bargains* and *puppy-dog glances*, the last

postures their living bodies
assumed—and we own him, have collected another
story in which a nearly
incomprehensible boy, one now impervious

to simple explanations,
enters a fear-flung classroom somewhere too much like here—
Pearl, Springfield, Red Lake, Blacksburg,
Jonesboro, Santa Fe, Parkland, Newtown, Columbine—

to create his own master
list. What are we to say? *Thus assembled*, the writer
writes, *objects in a list are*
always whispering into the ear of their neighbor.

Toxin

He sees her, and it almost makes him wish
For coral snakes, deathstalkers, funnel-webs,
Bruno's casque-headed frogs, scorpion fish,

Even the hackneyed stranger in a suit
Pointing a poison pen—complete with darts
Like dandelion seeds, but ouabain-tipped

And strong enough to stop a dozen hearts—
Demystifying her paralysis,
But when he gets home, there is only this:

His wife, balled up and wobbling like an egg
About to tip onto its oblong side;
A picked scab's blood-smeared brushwork on her leg;

A shattered snifter; dishes in the sink.
He thinks he doesn't know yet what to think.
He hovers over her, a parachute

Just opening, all wrinkles and resistance.
Staring at her as though to gauge their distance,
He wants a substance, something quick and brute

And definite, to be the reason why
Whenever he arrives she starts to cry,
Wants to believe that nightly, when he walks in

The door and notices the not-yet-clean
Kitchen, the broken-glass glints dangerous
As lights of distant cities, it could mean

She's just been bitten by some venomous
Invertebrate and, dying, yearns to hear
The steadied tone of voice he always talks in.

Intro to Media Studies

The rumor reached us through the usual channels,
Our bric-a-brac brickbattish email forwards
And hypernormal clickbait hyperlinks

And even, on occasion, word of mouth;
And whether it was just a bullshit warning,
A feverishly embellished fabrication,

Or some more real, more genuine war story,
The gist of it was everywhere the same:
Whenever the enemy captured one of ours,

They'd fit a rickety metal apparatus
Around the prisoner's forehead, a device
Half steel-cold sweatband, half bronze-heavy brace

With one suggestive screw, and every morning
The enemy would turn the screw just once,
Slowly threading it into the prisoner's head.

Maybe at first it stops at mild discomfort,
Faint pressure—after all, one turn is one turn—
But soon enough the screw bores into bone,

And then the pain begins. That daily turn?
We've heard it's called the Centimeter Scream.
Once freed, those men and women trot along

With metal bands around their heads and screws
Tunneling deeper, twist by detrimental
Twist, till the bluntest tips, at some point, touch

Brain tissue, which is where the damage starts:
Our pain will always be, if nothing else,
A form of prophecy. Those banded freak shows'

Cognitive functions warp and then diminish,
Depending where the enemy has placed
(With trained exactitude, with care) the screws,

Such placement being something of an art
Of theirs. We know what happens: memory loss,
Insatiable and better-left-unspoken

Desires, incessant bodily secretions,
New phobias, new loathings, new obsessions
With secret rituals or coded signs

All vaguely awful. What the best-placed screws
Do seizes us from sleep: those ghouls survive
For years and years and turn the screws themselves,

Harder and faster, fiddling with the heads
As though they were, with fearsome concentration,
Tuning into a favorite radio station.

Face the Music

Can we talk
about to face the music,
she texts me, not
because there's music to face
but because we're word persons—word nerds, even—
and love the unexpected
ripples and tangles of language. *Where does it*
come from, why would it be bad.
I envision an imperial throne room
silent except for the soft

insinuations of a septet of string instruments,
and before the emperor
fidgets some frantic
low-level functionary
about to discover which finger he will no longer
be needing, but since I'm next
to my laptop, the network in easy reach, I look it up.
The *OED*: "[Origin
uncertain and disputed: suggestions include reference
to a nervous performer

coming onstage in musical theatre, or to the practice
of drumming a soldier out
of his regiment (see DRUM *v.*[1]), or to
various military
uses of MUSIC *n.* (as e.g., senses 5
and 8c at that entry)],"
and being a diligent worder, I click on sense
5, which reads, "that component
of a military force charged with sounding signals
on musical instruments,"

and I think, *sure,*
   I wouldn't want to face that,
and then I jump
   to 8c: "*slang* (chiefly *Mil.*).
The sound of gunfire or other
   ordnance," and that's all it takes,
I'm thinking of what I've been thinking of for two
   days straight, the man who hammered
out his hotel windows and opened fire on a country
   music festival, killing

more people than any mass shooter in "modern
   American history."
So this is history. People thought
   the gunshots were sound problems
or fireworks. Some of them have now
   become numbers to the rest
of us, parts of an unimaginable sum.
   It happened in Paradise,
an unincorporated (at root: "unembodied") town
   near Las Vegas, a city

enamored of chance, one where you yank the same
   lever over and over,
forever hopeful that here, at long last, your lucky
   numbers will come up, your ship
come in, your cliché
   dreams come true, and despite how
often you lose—how far you are from ever
   hitting the bells-and-whistles
jackpot—you pull
   the lever, you play your hand,

your ship
   always seems almost in sight
of land, and in the midst
   of this it is probably
wrong to be angry at the aggressive stupidity
   of #heartbroken, now
trending in America, except that I am angry:
   the language, or what passes
for language, angers me. Can we talk
   about facing the music,

can we talk about the not-talking
   and the overtalkative,
the shouters-down, the shammers, the spin doctors,
   the czars of twittle-twattle,
can we talk about Twitter? Scroll down a few days and you see,
   "Video games are giving
guys unrealistic standards as to how
   many swords we can carry,"
and then, of course, "#heartbroken," because the language
   we use for video game

quips is the same
   language we use for human
massacres here in the bumper-sticker nation,
   home of the slogan shogun
with insights bound to wind up sound bites,
   harbor for the hair-triggered
trigger-happy captains of snappy comebacks—
   the woman I saw today
wore a black spaghetti-strap tank that blared
   OBAMA CAN'T TAKE THESE GUNS

just two days after.
   Our shootings are beginning
to feel like echoes—so many precede them—
   but unlike most echoes, these
aren't fading:
   they're growing louder, growing
stronger, sounds
   amplified after their first
report
   from some distant, unknown source.

Can we talk? The *Onion*
   publishes the same headline,
"'No Way To Prevent This,' Says Only Nation Where
   This Regularly Happens,"
every time this happens.
   Numbers keep ratcheting up
like a decibel meter reading: the world's too loud
   to hear. #heartbroken.
Gunfire. We're facing nothing. What we won't say is
   music to somebody's ears.

The Offering

The room is full of empty chairs.
The gods above break down, distraught.
We offer them our thoughts and prayers.

Later that week, the Law declares
In bullet points we've learned a lot.
The room is full of empty chairs

Persuaded by these solemn airs—
And those survivors? They are not.
We offer them our thoughts and prayers

While an explosive skeptic shares
Links proving this a deep-state plot.
The room is full of empty chairs.

"We've still got time if someone cares
To leave us with a final thought . . ."
"We offer them our thoughts and prayers,"

Some suit recites as he prepares
To squeeze off one last parting shot.
The room is full of empty chairs.
We offer them our thoughts and prayers.

Thirteen Ways of Looking at Anger

1

anger the starting
point the setting

out the site
wherein all one's

beleaguerments
begin anger

the *origo* the ur-
legend glossing

a madcap map
illuminated

as finely as if
by ink-tipped pin

anger the set
of unsettling

coordinates
making everything

icicle-clear
anger the arrow

pointing to anger
the text of

anger's aggrandizing
caption obviously

in red reading
YOU AREN'T HERE

2

anger like rock candy
hard jagged sweet

as I suck it
stuck by the sharp

prickles the pleasure
I note its unnatural

antithesis to mineral
savors of stones

rolling it around
my mouth

then crunching down
on what could be

of something small
maybe a bird the bones

3

anger the hanger
on which I hang

the trim black suit
I wear only

at home alone
sounding the mirror

with the black
patches punching

through gazing
at myself

evil-lipped
sneer-eyed

rehearsing
the moment

I plan to put it
and the whole

world on
buttoning

the one
button

and stepping
outside

4

anger the long
swig from a widow's

jug the held
back head

for a second
slug the bobbing

adam's apple
of every glug

then the crisp
gasp and thrilling

knowledge
the bottle

with every
swallow

is miraculously
refilling

5

anger the whetstone
anger the knife

anger the sound
of the one

sliding

against the other
the repetitious rasp

clink gritty scrape
anger the sound

stopping

6

anger the ten-
second
clip

I play
rewind
and play

catching
the studio
laughter

the clip's
quips
and savage

applause
echoing
for hours

after

7

the breath
I'm not taking

the bell
I'm not hearing

the beer
I'm still drinking

the bar
I'm clearing

8

anger the itch
I cannot help

but itch the bite
from some

little unthumbed
son of a bitch

I can't remember biting
me one wonders

what notions have
been planted what

plans have been
laid upraised

fist roar skirmish war
one wonders what

squirming larva
builds itself nightly

and when it will
hatch and whether

one will be the one
at the end

standing saying
no no no

it's just
a scratch

9

anger the odd
reflection in

the mirror the moment
some glint some all-

sufficient flash
blinds me into being

a man who can
only see the thing he saw

the moment
he stopped seeing

10

anger the sympathetic
listener sidled up

beside you
at the bar the host

of paralinguistic
cues and generous

nodding supporting
you in your views

with only the slightest
prodding that you

indeed have been
defamed disenfranchised

subjugated squashed
the one who

pulls back your chair

to help you
out into

the streets that soon
will know you're there

11

anger this stutter
splutter stammer

like the tentative
tappity-tap targeting

of a nail by a hammer
in a board too thin

for the hammer's hit
a necessary board now

irrevocably

split

12

anger the hit
single stuck
wormlike somewhere
undislodgeable

the mollifying
little melody
I whistle on
my walk to work

the beat I pound
on my steering
wheel while
bellowing at lights

the misheard lyrics
I mouth without
pretending
to understand

anger the riff
repeating in my head
the catchy chorus
and deceptive

cadence leading
into a crescendo
of feeling I'm shouting
skyward at top

volume awaiting
the redeeming
catharsis of one last
go at the hook

although without
the endless-seeming
budget or lush
production it's just

anger the radio
silence and round
about me dead air
and me me screaming

13

anger getting all
zen getting in

touch with its center
and the power

calm calligraphy
has to offer

watch anger
wrist and hand

tracing concentric
circles like a bird

beak in the water
watch anger

pinpoint the minute
it has finished

the brushwork
of this cool

bull's-eye
and begins

looking where
to pin it

• • •

More Furious, More Irrefutable

Latest fact: it turns out jet contrails aren't governmentally
dispensed psychotropic agents
bioengineered to turn the heartland American population gay or
autistic or whatever,

but, still, you can feel something barbing the air, a poisonous
atmosphere everywhere,
the clabbering of civility, the strange connections between
clickbait and road rage,

our immediate impatience almost tautologous as words of
ungulpable disgust go spilling
like mealy mouthfuls from overstuffed mouths in the war of
stuck-up cucks and stupid cocks,

all this tension an electromagnetic field one wanders into and out
of a dozen times a day.
We keep reading whatever feed fundamentally ratifies the version
of the world we want,

we keep imagining insults more furious, more irrefutable than
the ones we imagined
the day before, but mostly we are waiting for a future that, in its
cataclysm, satisfies

all of our longing for some vindication of this apocalyptic dread.
To have it be nothing—
to have the spurious claims and ramifying counterclaims reduced
to a species of pollen,

an irritant, to be sure, but mostly seasonal and ultimately little
more than a means
of some irrelevant, inhuman form of propagation—would be the
beginning of what

none of us could survive. Not yet unraveled and dissipated, those
cicatrix-like contrails
streamline the sky with cataracted redactions. Something cut,
something crossed out?

I sort with the thin-lipped factions who see a huge transparent
hand double-underlining
letters too large and clear to be legible in the giant invisible
sentence hanging over us.

Vectors

Less the shit-spurts or piss-floods of pure terror, crotch-cloth
darkening in brisk, eccentric, tectonically edged
          blots like an animated
          epidemiology

map that marks, in real time, the spread of an infectious
disease, and more the insistent low-grade tooth-grinding
          of moderate, strangely un-
          treatable anxiety,

the probative hollowed-out feeling of having found
cavities one can't brush away: the dread we had was
          omnipresent, like clothes in
          civilized society.

Our vectors of concern, definite yet infinite,
radiated from our chests like steel spokes from the steel
          hub of an immovable
          wheel, chaotic as the stays

and struts crisscrossing an amateur's summer garden;
follow any vector, and you would dead-end at some
          all-too-imaginable,
          amply televisable

fear: we might nuke ourselves, Crackberries gave us cancer,
our coupes were idly pulling down the sky one stoplight
          at a time. What would happen
          when, as per our worst sci-fi

fantasies, we could finally implant motherboards,
wires, widgets, you name it, directly into our brains
          and hear in ultraviolet?
          Download a scent? Cyber-tweak

on cyber-crank? Hence, the steel vectors radiating
from our chests: we looked like voodoo dolls, like overworked
          pincushions. Ice kept melting
          in polar caps and whiskey

glasses both. We let all the waves—radio, micro-,
Bluetooth, Wi-Fi—knead and numb our innards. Irony:
          we could never worry long
          enough in one direction

to be useful. Everything was fast, everything was
convenient, everything was done before we knew it.
          We envied the butterflies:
          through their bodies, the one pin.

Candidacy

That's a great point, Terry, but not one I want to talk about. Instead I want to focus on America's most pressing problem: dragons.

The science is in, Terry. Dragons are among us, with their impenetrable skin and unpronounceable names, blowing fire on hardworking single moms.

Their wings are huge—God, twenty, thirty times bigger than anyone imagined—and their eyes flicker like swamp-gas jack-a'-lanterns. They're taking our livestock, our lives, *our very way of life*—just eating us for breakfast, Terry, and that's not a figure of speech.

They have unintelligible names and are all but impervious to your average home arsenal: you'd have to own a, uh, a *bazooka* to protect your family, and even then, some of them just grow back new heads when you blow them off. Just grow them right back.

If climate change is real—and I'm not saying it's real, Terry, there's a very healthy, very active debate about that in the scientific community—I'd guess it's probably attributable to these dragons with their infuriating names blowing fire on hardworking single moms. I mean, you can't just burn America to a crisp like a rasher of bacon and expect it not to crank up the global temperature, am I right, Terry?

I read this one story—you can find it online yourself, it's on the front page of the internet—about a dragon with some brutish name literally swooping down on a hardworking single mom, snatching her baby right out of her arms, tossing it in the air, and bolting it down, one bite. I've seen the cell phone footage—I mean, it's amateur stuff: clearly, it's going to be blurry—

and I'll tell you, Terry, it just breaks my heart. It puts the fear in me. I'm not just feeding you a line: it ought to put the fear in *all* of us.

I know America's facing a lot of problems right now, Terry, a lot of problems with no easy solutions, but I think there's one thing the whole country, and especially its hardworking single moms, can get behind in these confounding times:

Kill the dragons. Kill the motherfucking dragons.

Long after Horace

What god can the people call as the Empire totters . . .
—Horace, trans. Rosanna Warren

Heaven knows—as the weeks accrete,
   Cancer-like, the irate cells of their days—we spend
Half our time on the internet,
   Skimming lists of the first symptoms of maladies,

Begging Google to find us feeds
   Blessed with accurate facts, snorting at random memes,
Same as always. We have a clear
   Motto: Best of all fates not to be bored. We aren't.

Still, and oftener than we'd like,
   Night arrives and our nerves jerk us awake. We scroll,
Calibrating our fears. We call
   Information a *flood*, frame as a *whirlwind* news

Cycling past in its fast-paced clips,
   Pluck some comfort from terms tying us back to earth—
There where dangers are agentless,
   Not like those we're afraid nobody made but us.

Yes, we've scuttled the quaint accounts,
   Unbelievable now—thinking the world could end
Wracked by earthquakes, tornadoes, droughts,
   All the ancient machines. Innocence had its charms.

Nowadays we imagine cracked
   Despots punching in codes, flanked by their renegade
Science-goons who've designed a germ,
   Gene, or cyborg with dream circuits to sort us out.

Worse yet, knowing the odds, we're still
   Synthesizing the best hormones to boost troops' bone
Strength, still titrating acids most
   Useful for the prolonged eating away of hope—

Perfect tools for the torture squads
   Knocking, briskly, on doors. Once, we'd have prayed to gods,
Bid them open the cloud-locked skies.
   Now we're writing concerned letters to men with ties.

Quarterly Report on Volunteer Participation

. . . nomination is the first procedure of distraction.
—Roland Barthes

First, all volunteers were
questioned on topics for which we felt
reasonably sure
we had accurate data—income, diet,
sexual preferences—to establish a baseline
for responsiveness. Most conversed
nervously and interspersed

their answers with questions
about acquaintances, providing
a convenient means
of redirecting inquiries toward our prime
concerns: their personal relations and areas
of expertise. For them to share
much at this stage was quite rare.

All volunteers agreed
to abstain from alimentation
and sleep, and thus freed
from distraction by external stimuli,
a few demonstrated an increased ability
for precise factual recall
after a brief interval;

however, most showed none
even after several straight weeks of
participation,
leading our staff to conclude other methods
of facilitating access to short- and long-term
memory were needed to show
volunteers how much they know.

Chemical trials were
selected by, or for, volunteers
to help us deter-
mine how serial injections might affect
the readiness of individuals to respond
to inquiries. This stratagem
worked on, or for, some of them

(twenty), but a number
of volunteers still demonstrated
a most peculiar
indisposition to factual recall
despite the encouragement of our professional
facilitators. (Some percent
of volunteers underwent

a loss of bodily
fluids, body mass, and at the worst
unnecessary
cognitive functions, the foreseeable side
effects of the chemical trials to which they each
agreed. See individual
signed-stamped release forms for all.)

For those volunteers least
able to recollect clear details,
we had to enlist
more specialized professional personnel
and undertake more experimental approaches
involving lively back-and-forth
before anything of worth

emerged. To start, many
volunteers chose the voluntary
onychectomy
to facilitate shared mnemonic access,
transmitting personal relations' areas of
expertise item by item
at more-than-ample volume.

Fittingly, reluctant-
to-speak volunteers who understood
their state underwent
maxillofacial reorientation
and subsequently managed to access short- and long-
term memory (and could transmit
their information by writ).

Certain voluntary
electro-papillary treatments
boosted memory
capability in volunteers (voltage-
rate graphs attached), but often we had to modify
a small part or parameter
to streamline the procedure.

Seamless improvising
grew de rigueur: we had to devise
exciting cutting-
edge methods to help volunteers recollect
the facts we lacked. We succeeded because we practiced
the secret to any art, theme
and variation, on them.

Here we ought to mention
that we consider our one hundred
percent retention
rate conclusive proof our program addresses
some fundamental need in citizens, which is why
they continue to volunteer
year after year after year.

Obligations

How awful they can sound, like weekend chores,
        So primly Latinate
    And obstinate the obligations
        One naturally abhors
        And more or less can't wait
To pass down to the upstart generations

        Like heirloom silverware
Or global warming, debt or doing dishes;
    And yet—at root, seen through—they're ties,
Kin to the latticework that backs a chair
Or stitcheries that bind our wiles and wishes
        In books we canonize,

And there'd be no immortal tapestries
        To sanctify a space
    Without the back-and-forth of looms—
        No complex harmonies,
        No lovers who enlace
Their fingers down the aisle as brides and grooms,

        No healing ligatures,
Not one religion to redeem the times . . .
    Indeed, our very DNA,
Composed of double helices, ensures
Our subtlest chemistries must find their rhymes.
        What more is there to say?

Behold the weeping woman who would bring
        The costliest libation
    Or weave long promises of prayer—
        Who'd give most anything—
        For one more obligation:
The nightly braiding of a young girl's hair.

The Magician Contemplates Certain Mysteries

But in the end
Any protection would have to come
From Providence, him-her-or-it-self, working
By whatever hidden means usually employed,
Which we know to be so secret and so various.
—John Hollander

Children love magic: dollars ripped in half
And pyrotechnic pigeons make them laugh.
Why wouldn't they? The birds return to sender,
The bucks get stitched back into legal tender,
And every quantum quarter reappears
From somewhere just behind jug-handle ears.

These mysteries, though latent, must be learned,
As masters of the craft have long discerned.
Charming a stick into a harmless snake,
Repairing pairs of spectacles you break,
Conjuring silk scarves in concatenation—
You start with simple prestidigitation,

And even then, scoffers can't quite explain
Some feats of your alleged legerdemain:
No hands could move so fast, nor fingers flick
So quickly, as to render every trick
Explicable. Thus, gawkers watch, wide-eyed,
Boxed sidekicks sawn in two while you decide

Which laws of physics break. You can produce
Absinthine blurs of fire with your abstruse
Imperatives or make kids' thoughts converge
On one card, picked by you, the thaumaturge,
Or levitate or, with a mock blown kiss,
Induce that fleeting faux paralysis

That locks a volunteer's feet to the ground
Or even choose to let yourself be bound
In serpentine, cocoon-like coils to prove
No ties too binding—you can hardly move,
Contorted into that inhuman shape.
You still break free. To play up your escape,

You let them tie the knots with their own hands.
You know the ropes: how one large breath expands
Your ribcage, loosening the binds you're in,
That you, like Daniel, may step into the din
Of their acclaim. You smile from ear to ear,
You take your bow, and then you disappear.

Who am I kidding? All magicians know
These acts are parlor pastimes and children grow
Into the painful knowledge palmers tried—
With every slick, distracting trick—to hide.
Given this world, its weals and woes and welter,
Small wonder *subterfuge* once meant a shelter.

The best illusions end. No matter how
Many bouquets slip from my sleeves right now,
One day those kids will need to look beyond
The stopgaps of a top hat, cape, and wand.
What can I promise then? Their separate griefs
And hidden pockets full of handkerchiefs.

Let Me Correct You

1

Witness the kid, sweat-browed, test booklet yawning
Before him like a pulpy mouse-gray mouth,
Take stabs at vocab words—*betroth, behemoth,*
Euthenics—scribbling in the Scantron sheet
Whose empty bubbles call to mind the rush
Of trapped air that escapes a sinking fleet,

Then notice all the wall-pinned crayoning
Since this is kindergarten; hence, the crash
Comes swiftly. Kids are slipping into tears
And snapping No. 2s in half, they're wetting
Their pants and quaking in their plastic chairs,
They're winging Pop-Tarts pieces through the air

In protest, and their teacher—she who wearies
Of monotoning through the scripted shtick
The state curriculum requires—stands waiting
For moms: the kids are texting them a series
Of panic-thumbed emojis (why use words
When you can send a string of smiling turds?),

And soon enough the local news is panning
The room and lobbing questions ("Kids got *sick?*")
While sorting through the specialists' reports
(Stress levels in the seven-year-old cohort
Cringing through calculus and baby molars
Approximate an air traffic controller's),

And sure, you feel a little scorn, some spurts
Of what-the-actual-fudge, a smidge of just-
How-hard-is-it-to-scribble-in-a-bubble,
Except it's clear from all the teachers' test
Booklets with puking-student protocols,
Them little lettered answers might spell trouble.

2

Outrage blooms online like fields of bruisewort,
Whole ecospheres of digital indignation
As parents clamor for some saner means
Of granting kids a pain-free education,
And after months of front-page back-and-forth
About what knowledge costs and what it's worth,

The citizens in eager droves all come—
Beguiled now by their Golden Age—to drink
From the holy fountain of curriculum
Reform, results not being what you'd think:
The children fribble out of doors, their braids
Spinning like particolored pinwheel blades

As they unwisely cartwheel or whirl in place
Right after the organic bouillabaisse
They slurped for lunch (despite op-ed opining).
One toes an eastern racer's burst remains;
Others coerce the playground's roundabout
Into a centrifuge. Two bullied boys

Who miss their books achieve a moving balance,
Their unsuspected teeter-totter talents
Briefly the subject of their grade's regard
Before a crinkle of foil blows through the yard.
At last, behold our peace-and-plenty vision:
A troupe of children chanting in a ring

Around some common flowers none can name
While others mumble, racked by imprecision,
Still trying to remember what the game
With ropes and jumping is. Hop rope? Jump thing?
They wander free. They pace a vacant lot,
Untroubled by a single troubling thought.

Thirteen Nearly Identical Dr. Seuss T-Shirts

Somewhere in the distant, indifferent future,
once we have rectified probabilistic
and deterministic models through the use
of some presently unimaginable
equation—a dazzling combination
of biochemical micromodeling
coupled with advanced neuroplasticity-
  media interaction studies,
    an ounce-
    for-instance
    balance
  of how many sour-cream-
and-onion Pringles against how many hours
of *Criminal Minds*—someone will be able

to explain why I can't see a microvan,
regular van, sports van, box van, minibus,
or even brand-new Mercedes-Benz Sprinter
shined to a high polish, the windows tintless,
without a brain-marquee displaying *MOBILE
KILL STATION*. Oldsmobile Silhouette, stoplight,
left turn lane: mobile kill station. Ford Windstar,
  lit Walmart parking lot: mobile kill
    station.
    Chevy van,
    HEAVEN
  AND EARTH PLUMBERS stenciled
on both sides, clear view of all tools and total
lack of victims within: mobile kill station.

It's as though all the middle-class psychopaths
across America are traipsing around
with chainsaws and tarps and box cutters and dead
bodies and I'm the only one seeing them,
the only sucker savvy enough to know
every van is another van the world needs
to stay away from. When a ponytailed mom
    comes rattling back to the Walmart
        Windstar,
        one caster
        on her
    cart making the steering
jittery, it means nothing. Last week news broke
of the couple that held their thirteen children

captive for years, sometimes chaining them to beds
where they had to shift and turn and finally
give up on growing comfy in their own shit,
and now the Internet buzzes with pictures:
the hunched children, their faces protectively
blurred; the flabby, maggot-faced father, his lame
hippie haircut like a Lego clamp-on wig;
    the straight-from-your-nightmares, sunken-eyed
        mother,
        her gray hair
        and glare
    witchy as you could want.
In one picture, she looks like nothing so much
as a greater death's head hawkmoth with its wings

closed as she peers out of the helmet her head
has become; in another picture, famous
now, she's smiling. In court. How many warnings
do we give children? Don't talk, don't get too close,
don't take the Starburst, never get in the van.
The greater death's head hawkmoth is also called
the bee robber: it loves honey, it "mimic[s]
    the scent of honeybees" and thereby
        can have
        whatever
        the hive
    might offer of sweetness—
access breeds success—and still I'm thinking less
of the rare breaking-and-entering species

of kidnapper who zip-ties a father's wrists
together, inhabiting his new stolen
home for weeks while having his way with the whole
family before taking them, one by one,
out back to his mobile kill station, and more
of this woman who dressed all thirteen children
in red Dr. Seuss T-shirts, let them shower
    once a year, and starved them until her
        oldest
        (who'd have guessed?)
        "weighed just
    eighty-two pounds." She was
twenty-nine. Their gag tees labeled them Thing 1
to Thing 13. I like to daydream those beasts

let them watch at least enough television
to know their handcuffed home life wasn't normal—
enough to learn, rerun by saccharine crime
drama rerun, the ropes: deactivated
cell, 911, cops. I like to think their case
one of few, but their Wikipedia page
includes a link ("List of child abuse cases
    featuring long-term detention") that
        would take
        but one quick
        mouse click
    to open, and the page
that pops up would have links to, what, twenty more
pages, and I think: it doesn't have to be

mobile. Don't even need to kill them. Sometimes
it's enough just to keep things the way we do.
Officially, it's called *Acherontia*
lachesis: the greater death's head hawkmoth is
named for the Greek fate that measures out your life.
It smells, to honeybees, like honey, like home.
And that couple? They're everywhere still: Reddit,
    Facebook, Twitter, subject to hundreds
        of views
        the late news
        might use—
    shock-schlock we'll only see
if we sneak a nap in. What choice do we have?
Watch it, we tell children, who watch it happen.

PSA for the NRA

The sagas tell of one man known as "the children's man" . . .
—Peter Ackroyd

And lastly, let us glance
At a medieval tale
In which the hero's stance,

Not his war-warped stunts,
Will tell us how to feel.
A Viking warrior once

Was called "the children's man"
When, for the commonweal,
He broke ranks with his clan,

Spearheading this advance:
He chose not to impale
Children on his lance.

Songs of Power

Only the powerless sing songs of power.
The powerful content themselves with things
Other than song: the midday whiskey sour,
A smoke, the thousand bucks that every hour,
    Like luck's own lackey, brings.

They have no need for protest posters waved
Above the pates of some like-minded crowd—
They'd rather savor the pâté they've saved
For brunch. Their plaques, so tastefully engraved,
    To them seem plenty loud.

While powerless squirts form a human chain,
The powerful squint and line up big-league shots.
They snooker slack-jawed marks. They glug champagne,
They lap up sex. They know which gods ordain
    Their jackpots at the slots.

They smack lips, suck teeth, moan, and swallow whole
Whatever worlds they've figured theirs by right.
They rarely wonder why complete control
Feels incomplete. Askesis feeds the soul;
    Power, the appetite,

And appetite, like grief or grace, abounds—
How, with such hunger, can the strong stay strong?
Thank God those powerful slobs packed on the pounds,
And when they eat each other raw, it sounds
    As beautiful as song.

The Old Regret

. . . the beautiful changes
In such kind ways . . .
—Richard Wilbur

Sporting their spangled glasses
And dangling massive purses
From arms the texture of dried apricots,
The wives anatomize their losses
In one dyspeptic squawk that pierces
The pops of tennis rackets

And coughs as golf carts pass
While husbands, old and bored
With all the gabble, scan the tennis courts
In search of what? A pinch of spice?
A glimpse of fresh thighs, tanned and bared
In spurtful flouncing skirts?

Sometimes I think those old
Grubbers would have the young
Revere their bodies more as studied relics
Than relished selves: with half-concealed
Reproach, there's Gramps heel-rocking, yawning,
Checking his studded Rolex

As though he weren't still watching
That boy and girl play tennis
Like prom-tense partners cranking through a dance.
Her sweatband, snow-white and bewitching,
Half-holds her hair in blonde festoons.
The boy is your typical dunce.

Yes, older men would rather
Dispense like tranquilizers
Their knowledge of bodily failure and the folly
Of hope to every last mouth-breather
Whose muscles—as with all these losers—
Keep working beautifully

Because they do: fists grip
And knees, uncrepitant,
Bend freely; shoulders rotate; valves contract
With ease. The pipsqueaks never gripe
They have to take it slow, be patient—
For them, the thought's the act.

Surely the young must sense
Deep in their dream physiques
The heat, the asphalt shimmer, the love-all score
That renders them in our senescence
So satisfactory for sex,
So suitable for war.

Gridlock (You Aren't Going Anywhere)

After a teleconference
during which half a dozen
telefaces kept televying
for your attention, you double-click
on your social life (okay,
social *media* life) and update
your latest uploadable
moods, memes, and matters of importance,
then send to sleep your high-speed
firewalled connection to the real world
and beeline for the elevator—
which records you going down—
and hoof it out the building

(through the metal detectors,
past the six discrete discreet
security cams glaring at you)
and into the parking garage where
two drivers both on smart phones
back out of their reserved company
spots and into each other,
and once you've nestled into your car,
you plug in your down-and-out
iPod and when it won't work, turn on
satellite radio and tune in
to an all-talk station—more
chatter that doesn't matter,

a crackling background blur
that almost always soothes you,
though today it doesn't—while you zoom
toward the gym, taking care in your post-
workweek hurry not to run
even one of the half a dozen
stoplights on the way (stoplight
cams would have tickets in your inbox
before you'd finished your post-
workout shower), and once there, spandexed
and scrunchied up, you lope along on
an elliptical machine,
one in a uniform row

of elliptical machines
lined up in front of a row
of televisions, all closed-captioned
and turned to different entertainment
channels, and after a quick
rinse and a gridlocked bite in the car
on your way home (the takeout
place on your route takes plastic, praise be),
you arrive *chez toi*: a sheaf
of offers addressed to your old friend
RESIDENT, plus some half a dozen
more addressed to you by name
from people and nonprofits

you've never heard of, the bills,
a newspaper you don't want
to read (although, in fact, you were just
about to opt for a digital
subscription: your e-reader
currently bears a furring of dust)
because God knows what's inside,
then the sporadic, red attentions
of your answering machine
with its half a dozen messages
blinking their collective evil eye
(sometimes you're like that, old-school,
the sort that has a landline),

and when, at last, you turn on
your jank laptop (the webcam
light won't turn off) to check your email,
a pop-up for a paparazzi
candid shot that makes your spine
tighten and your ribs hitch pops up first
and, weirdly, that's it: you're done.
You need to go. You open your front
door and chuck your cell phone out
into the shrubs (good shot, good riddance),
then you unplug every appliance
in your house like an angel
of mercy making her rounds.

You clatter out the back door
   and into the woods that were
one more selling point and partly why
you took out an unmanageable
   mortgage to live here. You walk
down the trail you've always known was there
   but down which you haven't walked
till now. You feel it all receding
   like the studio fade on
a hit single you've never cared for—
goodbye banking app, goodbye burglar
   alarm, goodbye bajillion-
   bit reality, goodbye.

   The woods sizzle with silence,
   shiver, crackle twiggily.
Somewhere a bird chirps much like your phone
receiving a text or your coffee
   pot when it's hot. Then it's there,
a bird—what, a mockingbird? magpie?—
   the likes of which you've never
seen (but could you name half a dozen?),
   beautiful, to be honest,
and when it lands on a branch near you
and opens wide for song, you see in
   its mouth the momentary
   glare of a camera lens.

Performance Anxiety

Because we grew up fast
And digital, we knew
Of nothing that we couldn't do on camera:
Sob for pop-stars, foist
Our foibles on the few
Who watched our webcams, threaten. Cyber karma
Would only last a night.
Our psyches formed one hyperlinked chimera
We'd captured with a net.

Of course, the derrière-guard
Disputed our decisions,
Our freedoms, our unmediated selves,
Scared that we might be scarred
By all our live chat sessions
And video blogs. *What web connection salves*
The wounds of loneliness?
Those two-bit links will make you techno-slaves.
We listened less and less.

We stripped, we danced, we broke
Down. One girl cinched her neck
With a black belt and, pupils strangely dilated,
Let users watch her choke
Until her mother's knock
Clipped short the broadcast; we were most delighted.
Don't treat your acts like files—
Your memories can never be deleted,
They warned us. They were fools.

You're more than programmed drives;
Take care what you create.
They dreaded that we might do something *wicked*
In cybernetic droves—
Rage, self-destruct, run, riot—
And they were wise to worry when we clicked.
The plan grew bit by bit
As we kept thinking, thinking hard, and we could
See ourselves doing it.

To Keep the Day

What can we say? It took so little time
There at the end: we watched a record earthquake
Bury schoolhouses full of silent children,
Three hurricanes demolish our vacation
Spots—hectares of trees flattened like slicked hair,
Cities in the Atlantic half-Atlantised—
And epic wildfires conflagrate a state
To slideshow pics of slag-gray parks on *Slate*,
And those were just the isolate disasters,
Ones we were glad weren't happening to us.
Our autumn bottomed out at ninety-plus
Degrees that year; we died from eating lettuce
And spinach, apples, cheese, and milk; we shot
Each other with our stockpiled guns for reasons
As elemental as inclement seasons;
We even had an asteroid near miss—
"IT COULD IMPACT NEXT YEAR!"—as though all this
Were not enough, as though we didn't know
What this all meant when emptily we watched
A paper bag elected president.

But there were things to do: diverting apps,
Web recipes for perfect Caesar wraps,
Hot singles trends on iTunes and on Tinder,
A Netflix mail-bomb flick (*Return to Cinder*)
Rotten Tomatoes called "both dull and tasteless,"
Bevies of beauties—clothesless, witless, waistless—
To aid in masturbation, and our regnant

Divas so publicly, divinely pregnant . . .
Is it a shock with so much on our hands—
The flash mobs to promote our favorite brands,
The BOGO drinks at joints with open mics—
We flailed? So little life, so many likes.
We googled "moon like blood." We skimmed the hits.
Our search results had strange prerequisites,
And though we double-clicked on "The End of the Age,"
We only made it partway down the page.
We saw it all—that was our paradigm—
But we saw everything, and all the time.

What else was there to do? The night before,
We toggled our alarm clocks from the news
To triplicated beeps, popped one more beer,
Made sure to bolt the door, and went to bed
When we no longer could resist the yawning.
We'd get the gist by reading the reviews.
When that day came, to keep that day from dawning,
We stirred and chose the last thing we could choose,
Glad—grateful, even—someone had designed
A be-all, end-all button. Groan. Stretch. SNOOZE.

Make Jesus Great Again

Jesus considers: whores. His friends are whores.
        And fatties. Lushes. Sinners.
His followers, once tallied, feel outrageous:
The blind tripping, the legless blocking doors,
The deaf-mutes bleating. Not exactly winners.
Jesus reflects: is being lame contagious?

How did this happen? Jesus blames his mother,
        Too willing to accept, oh,
Anyone, really—weirdo, spaz, freak, geezer,
The whole stock-dropping bunch. *Just love each other*,
She murmurs, moved to welcome creep and klepto
And render kindness as such spirits seize her.

J. wants to hang with starting quarterbacks,
        Rock icons, soap soubrettes,
And shapely, fur-coat-swaddled socialites,
Wants to be better branded, wants thick stacks
Of C-notes, leather seats, one post that gets
A "Nailed it!" and a loft in Brooklyn Heights—

What else? New teeth. Tight abs. Instructive hair.
        He wants silk ties, chic glasses,
Some camel wingtips, swank from sole to eyelet.
He wants to rise to jet-set zillionaire,
He wants to soar above the harried masses—
A star, a god. Should all else fail, a pilot.

Amazing Selling Point

> *A blend of the finest Clove, Lemon, Cinnamon, Eucalyptus & Rosemary. Developed according to the legend of the four thieves in 15th-century England who used these and other aromatics to protect themselves while robbing plague victims.*
>
> —*aromatherapy oil bottle*

This proprietary blend of herbs—spearmint, fennel,
shankroot & ginseng—was steeped to instill an alert
feeling during chill night-long vigils when waylaymen
waited to ambush the parades of orphans being
transferred between nunneries, & these hand-sharpened knives
benefit from ancient techniques devised to perfect
implements of war that could sliver meat from the bone
more finely than a single-haired brush renders a line,
& this roots-&-spices dry rub—so secret the names
can't be listed—was refined over generations
to ensure human flesh was not merely edible,
but, well, nummy nummerkins. Here's a god who bites it
before the end of the book. Here's a heart so fragile
the fabric of it tears whenever Blink looks at Blank.
Here's an atmosphere so permeable you can bore
right through it by feeling dorky in bicycle clips.
The superior curvature of this strange posture
was first demonstrated near-simultaneously
by three different demographics: poor people stooping
to pick windfall peaches from a landowner's orchard
by night, poor people compressing like accordions
in landowners' mines to gather soundlessly clawfuls
of coal & poor people leaving landowners' houses

by the back door like little scurrying question marks.
These spirits, distilled from a now extinct subspecies
of amaranth grain, are used to strengthen the homemade
potions granting their modern-day occultic drinkers
power to force bare hands into the chests of victims
& remove vital organs—liver, lungs, heart—the way
Blink does just by looking at Blank. Here's a rare perfume
that permeated the room where they cleaned the body
of someone there was no deceit in: sweet hints of fig.
Here's a god so big he's unafraid to be eaten.

The Cards

The game's cards were about the size of coasters,
White 3x3-inch squares on glossy cardstock
With writing in two separate alphabets:
One, used for headings, was a modern version
Of something foreign yet familiar, something
Like the elaborate cursive scripts we'd stared at
On the first pages of the Gideon Bible,
Which promised us salvation in languages
We'd never even heard of; the other was
Our plain old Roman alphabet, so known
As to be basically invisible.

As was the game, completely camouflaged
By its ubiquity like those squat block buildings
Whose purposes and provenance elude one.
Who first began to pay attention to it,
Reading the lengthy bulleted instructions
On all the cards, the print surprisingly fine
And orderly? Who was the first to grow
Concerned at what it said? What sort of game
Had slowly, imperceptibly appeared
In all our homes—a warping of charades?
A strange role-playing game for dreamy misfits?

If so, it was a violent one, one no one
Seemed to be playing since no one ever saw
The game in action, just the game as presence,
The little stacks of cards so helter-skelter

The decks' edges seemed crazily serrated.
When someone who, we all believed, should know—
Some ludic specialist, some amateur
Cryptographer-philologist—discerned
They weren't a game, the neighborhood grew quiet.
We felt the air condense, coagulating
Into a clingy scrim like plastic wrap,

And everyone kept walking through it gently
As possible, afraid to be the one
To tear it now that everyone had learned
The game was not a game: they were instructions.
We couldn't tell from whom; nor *for* whom, really;
Nor could we make out when they would begin
The bulleted-list litany of violence
We'd read in passing when we read the cards
At all, but this we knew: the boldfaced headings
In that unrecognizable old language
From which we wove the fabric of our fears

Contained the signal at which it all would start.
Although none dared to speak of it, we wondered:
A secret broadcast over hidden channels?
A klaxon? An encoded message published
Somewhere public yet mostly unobtrusive—
A crossword puzzle clue in Sunday's paper,
A billboard? A light somewhere, eerily green
And burning in the sky for hours and miles?
An automated download? Or was it programmed
Into the very genes—the chemistry—
Of those who meant, one day, to take us over?

We saw the usual spike in firearm sales
And surges in esoteric vaccinations.
Dreamcatchers and assorted folklore-kitsch
Blossomed on front gates, porches, padlocked doors.
We didn't think to burn the cards or find out
Where we ourselves had gotten our own deck.
We grew obsessed with just one thing—the signal—
Although some wondered if we'd even notice
Should the prescribed invasion have begun
Already, silently, in steps that no one
Would recognize until they had been taken.

“i feel like a pot of scolding water on the verge of boiling over”

A flag flaps half-staff.
—Cathy Park Hong

The work so skillfully done, one almost fails
to notice the monotonous
undercurrent, the same sound at the center
of every word
and only the weak
schwa as variation. Straight A’s mean something
new now: sad, unsatisfying,

monotonous-turned-monstrous, and this morning
Colorado is on lockdown,
anticipating the anniversary
of Columbine.
The authorities
have even found a dead teen girl from Florida,
complete with pump-action shotgun

and self-inflicted wound. Her name, translated,
brands zeroes sky-high. Black T-shirt,
camouflage pants, black boots. She made “credible,
not specific”
threats. We’ve made neither
credible nor specific progress. She bought
three one-way tickets. Guesswork proves

hard. No matter where I start, I keep ending
up here: cut the deck, flip the card,
and staring you in the face is one lonely
heart reminding
you—by pip, by suit—
the better the marksmanship, the more likely
the shooter will be called an ace.

Why We Remember the Martyrs

"Forgive them, Father," Saint Stephen mutters, "for they know
    not what I'm about to do,"
and then he clamps his teeth down around the pin, pulls it,
and lobs the grenade (like a stone) at the gathered mob
    of persecutors. "This side
    is done," Saint Lawrence, being

grilled, growls, and when they flip him, there in his outstretched hands
    is a pair of well-oiled Glocks,
and he fires with the cool precision of an expert
marksman into the foreheads of the firebrands whose ire
    he'd so inflamed they'd held him
    over a real grill. And how

could we forget that nameless Roman human torch, tarred
    by Nero and set alight
to smoke out the remnant, who instead of suffering
in silence or singing hymns to the God he felt sure
    he was soon to meet, wandered
    into the Roman Power

Works facility and with his burning-but-not-yet-
    consumed body, in the most
self-sacrificial of righteous gestures, ignited
neighboring barrels of fuel, causing an explosion
    that decimated dozens
    of the surrounding Roman

blocks and their inhabitants and stopped power for weeks,
allowing the remaining
Christian martyrs to rally, regroup, relock, reload,
and return with full firepower the pagan fury
of the Roman emperor
on both him and his people,

mowing them down for the pleasure of God? Sebastian
with his Navy SEAL training
and crossbow, picking them off one by one. Agatha
lifting the rubber polymer faux boob to reveal
the bomb below. And, of course,
Martin Luther King, Jr.,

taking one last drag from his unfiltered cigarette
and then extinguishing it
in audible hissing fizzles against the stonework
of the tower where he squats with his sniper rifle,
the scope now pressed to his eye,
delivering his famous

one-liner—quoted forever after though always
wrongly and out of context—
in a whiskey-soaked voice of hard-won knowledge: "I had
a dream." We celebrate them all, God's little flowers,
jeweled sundews in that garden
where traitors hang from branches,

and know where they belong: on cheap keychains, on T-shirts
where their carefully airbrushed
faces, bellicose though embellished, blaze unfaded

no matter how often we wear them, on belt buckles,
    on a pricey pigeon-gray
    limited-run pair of cleats,

on bedroom posters sporting a motto that captures
    the *casus belli* in words
wound from twisted barbed wire, and—to help them sleep soundly,
wrapped in the myth—on the patterned pillowcases, sheets,
    and synthetic comforters
    we cover our children with.

Talking Heads

Behind the chatter
of full-blast shower water,
I hear the swift tick

of one steady drip
ricochet off the faucet
with an implicit

impatience, one quick
with something more sinister:
who has never heard

at a drunk mixer
a room-vaulting snicker crack
the background gabble,

nor sensed in current
events some fait accompli,
some calculated

score, one strategic
leak in what would be the last
week before the war?

Mulberries

A third of the way through our thirty days of lockdown
replete with pandering
                                        pundits and stock-shock headlines

and oscillating estimations, estimations
oscillating like a manic hand
                                        holding a hand-
saw sawing through the same branch we're creaking shuddering
swaying shaking on, I take
                                        my daily outdoor walk,

a last link to pre-pandemic sanity and one
that gives me time
                                to think—about the fact A MAN THOUGHT
SOMEONE LEFT A BOX OF PUPPIES ON HIS LAWN, which seems
bait-and-switchy since
                                        the headline continued, NOPE, THEY
WERE BEAR CUBS, or the fact that A GEORGIA BAR OWNER
REMOVED
                $3714

WORTH OF BILLS STAPLED TO THE WALLS TO GIVE TO HER UN-
EMPLOYED STAFF, or the fact that
                                                AN OREGON POLICE
DEPARTMENT IS ASKING RESIDENTS TO STOP CALLING
911 BECAUSE THEY'VE RUN
                                        OUT OF TOILET PAPER,
or the fact that every day there's another clapback

indignity, another
                    brink or lunk, another
TikTok video—and pacing neighborhoods, thinking
of it all, I can't describe how
                              weirdly glad I feel

to hear one kid in a tree proclaim to another
kid in the tree, *I'm drunk*
                              on mulberries. Well, half-drunk.

The Night I Finished Auden

The night I finished Auden
  Was much like any night:
A palatable meal had
  Appeased my appetite,
A sweating green-glass bottle
  Provided company
For Auden, in absentia,
  And absent-minded me.

I like the later poems,
  Mannered and talkative
With doctrinaire digressions,
  For posing how to live
Gracefully with the knowledge
  That even the most wry,
Intelligent, and gentle
  Among us, too, must die.

Wystan, you mastered meters
  For which I know no names
And thanked the god who gave us
  Our grammar and our games,
Then selflessly accomplished—
  A born iconoclast—
Your corpse, but left your corpus,
  Of which I've read the last.

I feel like one who's wandered
  Through hitherto unseen
Landscapes, equipped with nothing
  But compass and canteen
And tasked by ghosts with finding
  A form that could contain
An elegy for oceans,
  An epitaph for rain.

Infinency, Depressioners, Un-Existable, Tormentations, Existor, Perceivations

They strike me as the odd, archaic
Poeticisms plucked perhaps
From Renaissance prose stylists' *oeuvres*—
Lancelot Andrewes, Thomas Browne—
Or from the patent applications
Empurpled past all sense by some
Victorian pseudoscientist,

The mind behind the diplograph
Or spherical velocipede,
The way-back-when unknown inventor
Of the pneumatic stencil pen
And nearly of the spirit phone
(Purported to record the dead),
But they all come from diaries

By Dylan Klebold, hardly someone
Who needs another word. The book
I found them in has listed them
As symptomatic evidence
That Klebold had a schizotypal
Personality disorder:
The "fragmented thought processes,"

The fact that he believed "strange things"
And had "bizarre preoccupations,"
The "difficulty separating
Reality from fantasy"—
Yet now he sounds like nothing more
Disturbing than a turbid writer,
One of that tribe of pen-cap biters

Who suffer nameless tormentations
And promulgate their perceivations
Bromidic and bizarre. They cross
Lines, un-existable existors
Who flesh out their depressioners,
Their sole job slapping language where
Everything hurts. Everything hurts

When rage and anguish interface.
They seek "a timeless, spaceless place,"
A dreamscape infinency where
Our speechlessness grows limitless—
Somewhere where consciences are clear,
Where even straight lines meet, a place
That we can almost see from here.

Healing Leaves and Unimaginable Flowers

What other indignities
must I suffer flagrantly before I find the Just
City, the garden I left
before I was even born? Pull up the policies,
quote the terms of agreement,
provide me with tables of the precise point-value
breakdown before I break down

or out or up or through to
the other side of grievance because it's not so much
the indignities themselves
as the uncertainties regarding their relative
scoring: when I mispronounce
peony to rhyme with *pony*, stressing the long *O*—
like *crony, phony, stony*—

how many points do I earn?
When I ask the woman in the none-too-slimming black
dress when she's going to have
her baby, and she tells me four months ago, how much
is that worth? How much closer
am I to the long-promised prospect of healing leaves
and unimaginable

flowers? I picture heaven
as a Customer Service desk where polo-shirted
personnel with name badges
brocaded with the swoops and lags of a strange language
laugh and chat without ever
answering the bright red phones that ring without ceasing,
and I can take to them all

the unfulfilling moments
of my unfulfilling life—like some defective pair
of clunky VR goggles
weighting a white plastic bag twist-knotted at the top—
for a refund or exchange.
They don't ask for a receipt. They only want to know
if I am ready and when

I tell them I've been ready
my whole life, the phones stop ringing, the chatter snaps off,
they stare at me with something
between sadness and bewildered ardor and wish me
a good day and send me back
into the world, which is just what it has always been:
one big, beautiful garden.

Some Call It a Care Package, Some Call It a Sick Kit

It wasn't that she handed me a smudged-up Ziploc
 bag containing a travel pack of Kleenex,
some Lipton tea, a grubby card with kid-scribbled GOD
 IS LOVE on the envelope

and GET WELL SOON on the plain white wordlessness inside,
 a polychromatic handmade cardboard cross
composed of little hopscotch squares with exegesis
 ("White represents the cleansing

of our sins" and "Yellow represents God's perfect light")
 wherewith I imagined a tiny person
with a tiny stone skipping her way to salvation,
 plus three sugar-free cough drops,

which she did; nor even that she trilled, "Jesus *loooves* you!"
 the topmost grace notes floating her piccolo
voice, then tipping, then rushing down cadenzas of joy
 only a child is sincere

enough to express without the pedal tone of shame,
 which she did: it was that her face was nearly
incandescent when she said it, splendent like metal
 heated to the hammering

point, ready to ring with the spark-fringed blows of being
 shaped to the use of some smoky, muscular
intelligence, and for that moment I placed my trust
 in pure, potent mystery

although since then I've grown doubtful of certain details—
  it happened so fast, she handed me the bag
and said the words and was already skipping away
    like the vision of Zeno,

and suddenly I was old and so much time had passed,
  I was surrounded by family and friends
and strangers with masks and the small white room was beeping,
    and I could hear her speaking

in that voice I thought I recalled yet somehow didn't,
  and I saw her face and clothes both exceeding
white, glistering, whiter than snow, such as no fuller
    on earth could ever white them.

"☆☆☆☆☆!"

What I want you to understand, my dearest transhuman data patterns encoded
on quantum nanoprocessors locked in moisture-free
glass cases complete with sensors
to parse and disperse
whatever
space dust

might glitch your sensitive circuitry—what I need you to know, my hands-free apps, my brave
new wares, my brave nowheres, my lovely algorithmic
constellations of aughts and naughts—
is that the world changed
so quickly
no one

muddling through ancient meatspace understood what was taking place. One day we woke up
and every thought everyone had ever had had been
archived forever: searchable,
safe, accessible
to all through
snippet

view. Footage: every atrocity, every Taylor Swift goat-remix. Eight billion views.
Quantifiable likes, face-morphing filters, drop-down
emotions. Sound bites: each word, each
burp. We barely had
hard-drive room.
Nude pics

of our daughters spread like measles, everything could be rated.
We thumbs-upped what we called
a challenge: flinging Kraft Singles into the faces
of babies. We mastered the art
of the blistering
authorless
comment,

we savored bleach-martini memes. We loved body shots,
screenshots, hotshots, potshots. We snapped
dank selfies, our butt cheeks bunched on sink edges, our jaws
clenched for better definition.
Occasionally
we looked back,
stylish

with droll frames around what some figured windows to the soul.
All of it was happening
at once in six-second increments, in two-hundred-
character cerements. The world
saw itself disin-
tegrate, gave
itself

five stars, pressed forward. Can you even imagine? By now, you
probably don't have to.
You must live so fast my thought's speed seems pure broadband,
pure
nonsense. At least our dust was dust.
Listen: binary
once meant two
burning

bodies that would revolve, if not around each other, then around
their common center.
We pointed at constellations. Our stars were real stars.
We stored files for a familiar
future binge-watching
fails we called
epic.

Well, at Least They Got One Thing Right (Including 5.8% David Kirby, 3.1% William James, 2.4% Bad Ninja, 1.8% Andrew Marvell, .6% Lee Van Cleef, .6% Jocular Lexicographer, and .1% Shakespeare)

. . . and even these movies often have a scene
or an exchange between two characters
or a word said a certain way
or maybe just a facial expression
that you'll not only remember for years

but use in a way that changes your life
for the better . . .

—David Kirby

Okayokayokay, so Lee Van Cleef—*Lee Van Cleef*—
turns out to be a ninja,
a noticeably, somewhat surprisingly, paunchy
ninja until he slips on
his ninja mask, at which point he inexplicably
quick-thins and spin-kicks the villainous other ninja
that has been shadowing him
forever in the '80s
series *The Master*, a show

that is—how do you say?—dismal, a hack job so rank
that two episodes of it
were Frankenstitched together, seams-be-damned, and treated
as a feature-length movie
by the *MST3K* crew, which specializes

in flopperoos a space-drudge and his robot puppets
    can pillory, in this case
    by needling, scene after
    scene, Lee's sudden slenderness,

and though most of *The Master* is facepalmingly bad,
    at one point, Grampa Lee snags
the arm of some henchman who says, "The old man hired you,"
    and Lee responds, "I am not
for hire," and the henchman, who is Lee's as-yet-unknown
nemesis, counters, "We are all for hire in dark times,"
    and I think, *OK, they got*
    off one *good line.* Or maybe
    not. Maybe I just like it

because my self-styled sense of selves—ethical, moral,
    epistemological,
tragical-comical-historical-pastoral,
    plus all -etic and -istic
adjectival permutations, as well as whether
one likes, on a given day, the singe of cinnamon
    or suffers stoplights nobly—
    changes, as we change, nightly,
    a stance useful insofar

as it is useful. A favorite word: useful. A word
    I've heard myself applying
like plastic explosives to friends' cockamamie plans
    or students' proposed courses
for Fall Term: *I'm just not sure*, I murmur ever-so-
wisely, *that would be useful.* Satisfying? You bet.
    Morally good? Meh, maybe.
    But useful? No, prolly not,
    and there deliberation

ends because, above all things, choices must be useful.
          Thus, I'm learning I might be
less a lapsed Christian and more a proto-pragmatist,
          although God knows what that means—
when I google "pragmatist," nothing useful comes up.
Even to think my faith might not be in higher things
          but simply up for hire,
          winnable by whatever
          ultimate concern will pay

the best dividends, turns my Inner Youth Pastor mute,
          but Rain God? Sure, if it rains.
A rabble of half-drunk gods and goddesses engaged
          in constant squabbles, throwing
benders and lightning bolts? Not great, but it would explain
a lot. Water-and-waves-style Zen, a cosmic ocean
          to which I'll one day return?
          Honestly, not my first choice,
          because as Andrew Marvell

notes, "The grave's a fine and private place, / But none, I think,
          do there embrace," of which, first,
ditto in cosmic oceans; and second, that "embrace"
          covers a heckuva lot.
"Grant an idea or belief to be true," William
James writes, "what concrete difference will its being true make
          in anyone's actual
          life?" Yeah, what does it matter
          that I slightly embellished

Lee Van Cleef's spin-kicking achievements for the worthy
          purpose of comedic punch?
That *The Master*'s best line, according to my buzzkill
          friend, is borrowed? That I use,

embarrassingly but indisputably, a few
too many adverbs? Lee's nemesis also declares,
"The night is always with us,"
and I feel it even now,
hovering on the other

side of the planet. One wit summed up pragmatism
in four words: "What works is true."
Someone else: "Mere expediency and low cunning."
As for Tiamat, that's what
I named the skink who used to skitter through my garage,
a rain-slick root vegetable pronged with legs: I meant it
as a sign of respect for
both lizard and deity
and, verily, who's to say

that this single act of defiance or deference—
whichever—won't be the one
that matters most? The working belief I need granted
true is clearly redemption
because there's, like, waaaaaay too much David Kirby in here,
yet who's to say one good line won't undo the bad ones,
the ones rattled off during
last year's hurricane-induced
blackout in an Applebee's

running on a generator, all thanks to the God
of Generators? And who's
to say the girl with amazing dreads won't take me home
because my one funny line
was the sole droll line she needed delivered? My whole
life I have been banking on the eyes-closed, held-breath chance
that at my baptism, when
the priest sprinkled my forehead,
one of those drops was holy.

Peace Riot

If his argument has about it the cold clockwork
inevitability
of tooth-to-tooth torque—here, he writes, is the steadily
accelerating parade
of school shooters who orate epic manifestos
on self-shot home videos
or those who, determinedly irate, cope by making
spreadsheets that tabulate names,
dates, means, and kills; here, the scholarly underpinnings,
the Granovetterian
model of riots wherein threshold after threshold
of violence stone-by-stone gets
crossed; thus, in sum, our slow-motion, decades-long cascade
of violence: one long riot—

then perhaps we must accept that paradigm as true;
yet if it is, if we all
have such thresholds—I will not pick up this brick, this brand,
unless ninety-nine others
before me have done so—then surely we have thresholds
of peace. Here's the rage-ragged
adolescent, gun-addled, who'll not be quieted
unless everyone else in
the world goes first; here's the fired factory-floor worker
who'll pick up his last paycheck
unarmed if eighty-five forerunners have; here's the hoard-
primed eco-pirate who'll stop
price-tagging bog-peat or ice sheets if preceded by
only a dozen others;

and somewhere, there's the epicenter, the pined-for flash
point, the one who, no matter
how many or few won't, chooses peace. The one who starts
the riot: the peace riot.
Good speeds, domino-like, from that one, reaching even
me. One hand holds a burning
town: the heft, the rough gray texture, of what may yet be
a thrown rock. I set it down.

Adult Party-Goers: August 15, 1929

He stands there, marigolds erupting from his fist,
   Wearing a sundress pocked with black-and-white
Spheroids like florid petri dishes, moon rocks, comets
   Suspended in the frozen space composed
Of fabric and photography; he smiles and holds
   A woman's hand, his blond wig crooked, black
Ribbon and bow askew, a comic string of pearls
   Swaggily dragging nearly to his belt;
And you can tell: the one drunk first, the one drunk longest,
   Life of the party, funniest man alive—
Or in the room, at least—and surely dead by now,
   As all these people must be dead by now.

Despite his saggy sundress, despite the woman wearing
   A pageboy hat and loosely hanging tie,
Cross-dressing is just a gag like all the outsized bows
   Or skirts hiked up, the halfway-up-the-calf
Or wrinkled-to-the-ankle socks, the lonely beanie;
   What gives away the theme are all the toys:
The model telephone, the wheel-flanked metal cannon,
   Two metal horses with their wooden wagon,
The wooden horse and rider and the three-piece train,
   The pair of dolls, the parasol, the drink

That someone holds because, of course, one can pretend
   To be a child for only oh-so-long.
Behind the crowd, two doors: the open one, the closed.
   It's August 15, 1929,
Mere months before the stock market will crash completely—
   When, legend says, men sailed like balsa wood
Airplanes from windows of the buildings where they'd made
   And lost their fortunes trading futures—

And what most draws the eye among these adults dressed
   As children is the woman in the center
Who contemplates her doll, a woman who's pretending
   She's still a child pretending she's a woman
Who'll one day want a child, convinced she could be someone
   Who wants to have what she already has.

Notes

"The Collectors" on page 5: The epigraph comes from Lia Purpura's contribution to *Ley Lines*, edited by H. L. Hix. The final quoted language comes from the same source.

"The Offering" on page 14: This poem is a response to the aftermath of the Parkland shooting.

"Long after Horace" on page 41: The epigraph by Rosanna Warren comes from her translation of Horace I.2, which appears in *Horace, The Odes: New Translations by Contemporary Poets*, edited by J. D. McClatchy.

"Quarterly Report on Volunteer Participation" on page 43: The epigraph by Roland Barthes comes from "African Grammar" in *Mythologies*.

"The Magician Contemplates Certain Mysteries" on page 50: The epigraph by John Hollander comes from "Black Mask."

"Thirteen Nearly Identical Dr. Seuss T-Shirts" on page 56: The story of the Turpin family (and the children subsequently dubbed The Turpin Thirteen) made headlines in early 2018. Quoted language comes from Wikipedia pages (sometimes in previous incarnations, sometimes quoting contemporaneous accounts) about the Turpin case and about the greater death's head hawkmoth.

"PSA for the NRA" on page 60: The epigraph by Peter Ackroyd comes from *Foundation: The History of England from its Earliest Beginnings to the Tudors.*

"The Old Regret" on page 64: The epigraph by Richard Wilbur comes from "The Beautiful Changes."

“Amazing Selling Point” on page 78: The epigraph comes from the label of the Medieval Legend Blend by Mountain Alternatives.

“‘i feel like a pot of scolding water on the verge of boiling over’” on page 83: The title, quoted in a *Washington Post* article, comes from what are purported to be the digital diaries of Sol Pais, the eighteen-year-old Florida girl who committed suicide in Colorado near the twentieth anniversary of the Columbine massacre. The typo of “scolding” for “scalding” exists in the original. The epigraph by Cathy Park Hong comes from “Ballad in A.”

“Mulberries” on page 90: Headlines here are real and come from a variety of sources.

“Infinency, Depressioners, Un-Existable, Tormentations, Existor, Perceivations” on page 94: The title’s list of nonwords (or neologisms) and the phrase “a timeless, spaceless place”—drawn from Dylan Klebold’s diaries—come, as does the quoted diagnostic language, from Peter Langman’s discussion of Klebold in *Why Kids Kill: Inside the Minds of School Shooters.*

“Some Call It a Care Package, Some Call It a Sick Kit” on page 101: The final stanza incorporates language from several translations of Mark 9:3.

“Well, at Least They Got One Thing Right (Including 5.8% David Kirby, 3.1% William James, 2.4% Bad Ninja, 1.8% Andrew Marvell, .6% Lee Van Cleef, .6% Jocular Lexicographer, and .1% Shakespeare)” on page 106: This poem owes a substantial, if initially subconscious, debt to “An Otherwise Mediocre Film” by David Kirby, which also provides the epigraph. The “jocular lexicographer” is Peter Bowler; his definition of pragmatism occurs in *The Superior Person’s Book of Words.*

“Peace Riot” on page 110: This poem responds to Malcolm Gladwell’s provocative essay “Thresholds of Violence.”

“Adult Party-Goers: August 15, 1929” on page 112: This poem responds to a photograph from the Burgert Brothers collection, currently housed in the Hillsborough County Public Library, titled “Neel Yent home, 3010 San Jose, adult party-goers posed in ‘Kid’s Party’ *[sic]* costumes: Tampa, Fla.” Descriptions are accurate; characterizations are fictional.

Stephen Kampa is the author of four collections of poetry: *Cracks in the Invisible, Bachelor Pad, Articulate as Rain*, and *World Too Loud to Hear.* He is a winner of the Hollis Summers Poetry Prize, the Theodore Roethke Prize, the Collins Prize, and the Florida Book Awards Gold Medal in Poetry. He has been a resident at Art342 and at the Amy Clampitt House. His work has appeared in *The Best American Poetry*. He has also worked as a musician and appears on multiple albums from WildRoots Records.

Also from Able Muse Press

Jacob M. Appel, *The Cynic in Extremis: Poems*

William Baer, *Times Square and Other Stories; New Jersey Noir: A Novel; New Jersey Noir (Cape May): A Novel; New Jersey Noir (Barnegat Light): A Novel*

Lee Harlin Bahan, *A Year of Mourning: Sonnets: (Petrarch) Translation; Advent and Lent: Sestinas and Sonnets: (Petrarch) Translation*

Melissa Balmain, *Walking in on People (Able Muse Book Award for Poetry)*

Ben Berman, *Strange Borderlands: Poems; Figuring in the Figure: Poems; Writing While Parenting: Essays*

David Berman, *Progressions of the Mind: Poems*

Lorna Knowles Blake, *Green Hill (Able Muse Book Award for Poetry)*

Michael Cantor, *Life in the Second Circle: Poems*

Catherine Chandler, *Lines of Flight: Poems*

William Conelly, *Uncontested Grounds: Poems*

Maryann Corbett, *Credo for the Checkout Line in Winter: Poems; Street View: Poems; In Code: Poems*

Will Cordeiro, *Trap Street (Able Muse Book Award for Poetry)*

Brian Culhane, *Remembering Lethe: Poems*

John Philip Drury, *Sea Level Rising: Poems; The Teller's Cage: Poems*

Josh Dugat, *Great and Small: Poems*

Gregory Emilio, *Kitchen Apocrypha: Poems*

Rhina P. Espaillat, *And After All: Poems*

Anna M. Evans, *Under Dark Waters: Surviving the* Titanic*: Poems*

Nicole Caruso Garcia, *Oxblood: Poems*

Stephen Gibson, *Frida Kahlo in Fort Lauderdale: Poems*

Amy Glynn, *Romance Language (Able Muse Book Award for Poetry)*

D. R. Goodman, *Greed: A Confession: Poems*

Carrie Green, *Studies of Familiar Birds: Poems*

Margaret Ann Griffiths, *Grasshopper: The Poetry of M A Griffiths*

Janis Harrington, *How to Cut a Woman in Half: Poems*

Katie Hartsock, *Bed of Impatiens: Poems; Wolf Trees: Poems*

Elise Hempel, *Second Rain: Poems*

Jan D. Hodge, *Taking Shape: Carmina figurata; The Bard & Scheherazade Keep Company: Poems; Finesse: Verse and Anagram*

Ellen Kaufman, *House Music: Poems; Double-Parked, with Tosca: Poems*

Len Krisak, *Say What You Will (Able Muse Book Award for Poetry)*

Emily Leithauser, *The Borrowed World (Able Muse Book Award for Poetry)*

Hailey Leithauser, *Saint Worm: Poems*

Carol Light, *Heaven from Steam: Poems*

Kate Light, *Character Shoes: Poems*

April Lindner, *This Bed Our Bodies Shaped: Poems*
David Livewell, *Pass and Stow: Poems*
Susan McLean, *Daylight Losing Time: Poems*
Martin McGovern, *Bad Fame: Poems*
Jeredith Merrin, *Cup: Poems*
Richard Moore, *Selected Poems;*
The Rule That Liberates: An Expanded Edition: Selected Essays
Richard Newman, *All the Wasted Beauty of the World: Poems*
Alfred Nicol, *Animal Psalms: Poems*
Deirdre O'Connor, *The Cupped Field (Able Muse Book Award for Poetry)*
Frank Osen, *Virtue, Big as Sin (Able Muse Book Award for Poetry)*
Alexander Pepple (Editor), *Able Muse Anthology;*
Able Muse: A Review of Poetry, Prose & Art (semiannual, winter 2010 on)
James Pollock, *Sailing to Babylon: Poems*
Aaron Poochigian, *The Cosmic Purr: Poems; Manhattanite (Able Muse Book Award for Poetry)*
Tatiana Forero Puerta, *Cleaning the Ghost Room: Poems*
Jennifer Reeser, *Indigenous: Poems; Strong Feather: Poems*
John Ridland, *Sir Gawain and the Green Knight (Anonymous): Translation;*
Pearl (Anonymous): Translation
Kelly Rowe, *Rise above the River (Able Muse Book Award for Poetry)*
Stephen Scaer, *Pumpkin Chucking: Poems*
Hollis Seamon, *Corporeality: Stories*
Ed Shacklee, *The Blind Loon: A Bestiary*
Carrie Shipers, *Cause for Concern (Able Muse Book Award for Poetry)*
Gabriel Spera, *Twisted Pairs: Poems*
Matthew Buckley Smith, *Dirge for an Imaginary World* (*Able Muse Book Award for Poetry)*
Susan de Sola, *Frozen Charlotte: Poems*
Barbara Ellen Sorensen, *Compositions of the Dead Playing Flutes: Poems*
Rebecca Starks, *Time Is Always Now: Poems; Fetch, Muse: Poems*
Sally Thomas, *Motherland: Poems*
Paulette Demers Turco (Editor), *The Powow River Poets Anthology II*
Rosemerry Wahtola Trommer, *Naked for Tea: Poems*
Wendy Videlock, *Nevertheless: Poems; The Dark Gnu and Other Poems;*
Slingshots and Love Plums: Poems; Wise to the West: Poems
Richard Wakefield, *A Vertical Mile: Poems; Terminal Park: Poems*
Gail White, *Asperity Street: Poems*
Chelsea Woodard, *Vellum: Poems*
Rob Wright, *Last Wishes: Poems*

www.ablemusepress.com

Printed in the USA
CPSIA information can be obtained
at www.ICGtesting.com
JSHW021158221023
50376JS00003B/89

9 781773 491561